YUNUS

ﷺ

and the

WHALE

WRITTEN & ILLUSTRATED

by

NOURA DURKEE

Yunus
peace be upon him
and the
Whale

Published by:
Tahrike Tarsile Qur'an, Inc.
publishers and distributors of the Qur'an
P.O.Box 731115
Elmhurst, New York 11373-0115
First U.S.Edition 1999

written & illustrated by Noura Durkee

Library of Congress Catalog Number: 98-061665
British Library Cataloguing in Publication Data
ISBN: 1 -879402-59-9

The Prophet Yunus ﷺ is mentioned in the Qur'an
in chapters 4:163, 6:86, 10:98, 37:139-148;
and as Dhu-n-noon (the man of the fish) in 21:87, 68:48-50.

Muslims always ask the blessings of Allah
on the prophets and some others whenever the name
of the person is mentioned. Blessings used in this story are:

ﷺ : 'alayhi-s-salam: peace be upon him

Yunus ﷺ lived in a beautiful city called
Nin-i-veh. It had large stone buildings
and gardens full of flowers.
High walls went all around it.
There were great big gates in them.

All day long the gates
were open. People came
and went with donkeys
and horses and camels.
They carried carrots
and wheat and eggs
from the farms into the
city to feed the people.
They carried out clothes
and pots and pans
and tools for the farmers.

At night the gates were shut.
No one could come in, and no one could go out.

The people in this beautiful city weren't very nice. They used to cheat each other. They used to steal. They were selfish. They were mean. Also, they forgot to thank Allah for their good life. They didn't pray.

Allah told Yunus ﷺ, His prophet, to teach these people. Teach them to be good, fair, and kind. Tell them to love each other, and tell them to remember Allah!

That job was not easy. Yunus﷼ had to go into the markets and talk to the people where they were buying and selling.

Don't hit those ladies!

Hey! Allah doesn't like arguments!

Stop gossiping!

Stop listening to gossip!

They didn't want to hear any of this at all!

The people didn't like this news.
They just wanted to make lots of money and
be left alone. "Who is this man?" they said.
"He's just someone like us.
What does *he* know?"

So they laughed at Yunusﷺ. They called him bad names. They got mad at him and wanted to fight.

He tried and tried, but nobody would listen. Nobody would listen at all.

Yunusﷺ became very discouraged.
"This job is too hard," he thought.
"Nobody can hear me.
They haven't any manners!
And they haven't any sense!
Allah wants me to do it, but I can't do it.
I think I'll leave. I'll go far, far away from these terrible people. I'll find some place that isn't anywhere. And I'll hide there where even Allah won't find me!!"

He went and he went until he came to the place where the boats were.
He found a nice boat.
The sailors were loading boxes and bags.
Other people were getting on.
He paid the captain and got on, too.
The captain was happy to have another passenger.

The weather was fine.

They sailed away into the sea.

Then all of a sudden,
the weather changed.
The captain looked at the sky.
"A storm is coming!" he said.
"How strange!
It was a clear day when we started!"

Look out!

Tie everything down!

Hold on tight!

The storm came. It was a big one!
Huge waves broke over the boat.
It rocked back and forth
and up and down.
Everyone was very scared!

"We're going to sink!" cried the sailors.
"This storm is not normal!
Allah sent this storm just for us!
SOMEBODY on this boat
has done something bad!
We must throw him into the sea
to save our lives!

Yunus stood up. He knew the storm was for him. He didn't want the ship to sink with all the people in it. He understood now that he could never run away from Allah.

"Here I am!" he said. "Throw me into the water and the storm will stop!"

The scared sailors grabbed
his arms and legs
and THREW...

He went flying through the air,

and...*SPLASH*...into the water!

Down,

down

down,

down

down

...down he sank until...

Swoosh!

A huge mouth came at him,
and the water washed him in,

kerplop!

There he was,
all mixed up with small fish
and other things,
in the bottom
of the stomach
of a
great
big
whale!

What did Yunus ﷺ think then?
Maybe he thought:

"Why didn't I die in the sea?

Why am I here?

It's hot inside a whale,
And squishy.

It smells awful!
Maybe I'm never going to get out.

But I'm not dead yet!"

"Allah has given me time
to be sorry.
He put me here.
He's the only One
who can save me.

O Allah! I was wrong.
Nobody can run away
from You.
A person should stick to his job,
not give up.
I'm very, very sorry!"

"There is no other god, just You.
Glory to You!
I was one of the people who forget You
and turn away from You."

"I'm really sorry. Please forgive me!"

Allah hears everything.
Allah heard Yunus ﷺ inside the whale.
He forgave him. Yunus ﷺ began to feel
the whale turning and going fast...

Everything got very mixed up,
shrimp and shells and seaweed
and Yunus ﷺ Help!

OH!

all tossing about
and then, suddenly,

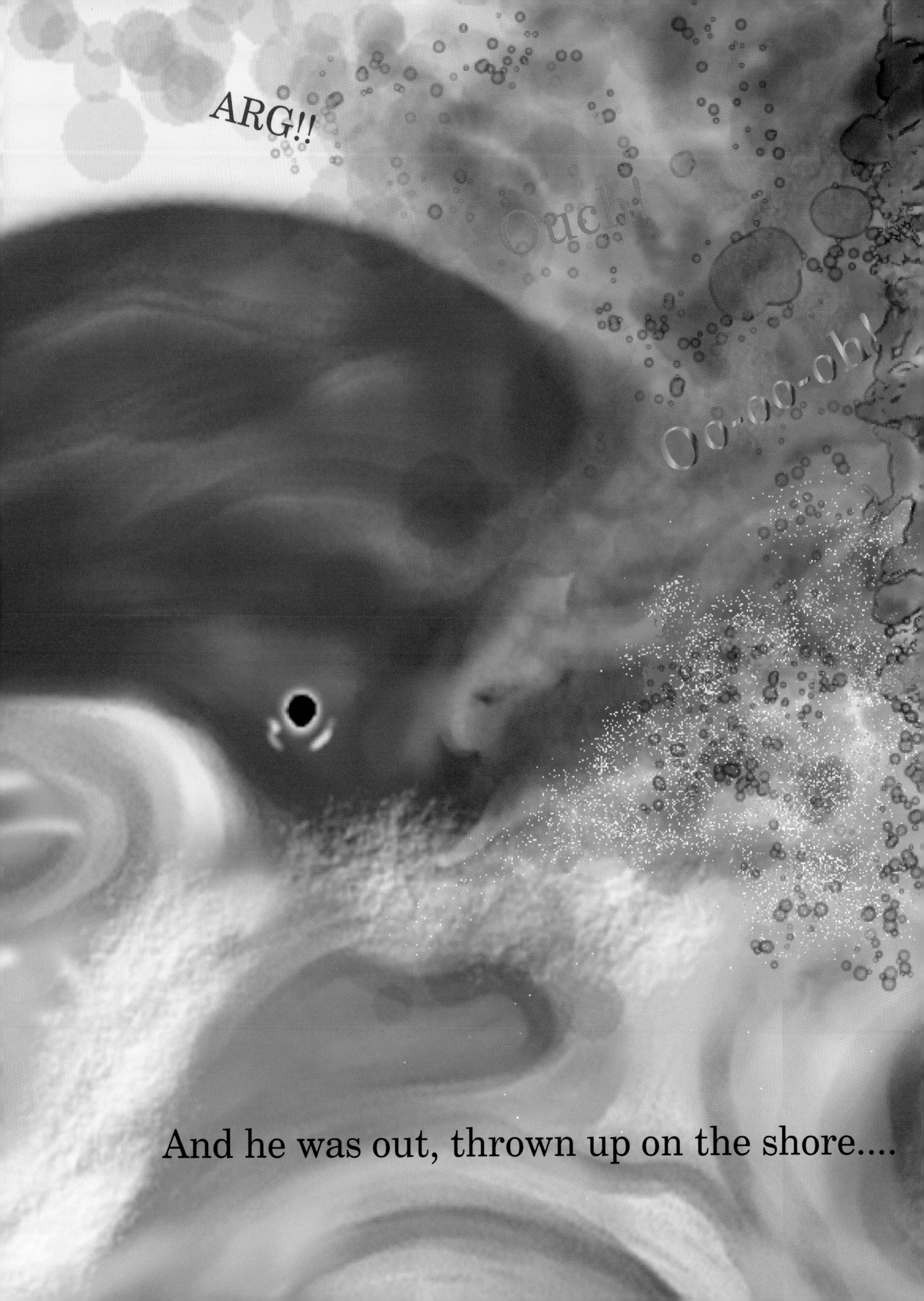

And he was out, thrown up on the shore....

...and he could feel the rough sand
under his body, and the whale was gone.

It was very light and very bright.
Yunus ﷺ was all wet and white and
soft from his ride inside the whale.
He was like something you might find
under a rock. The sand was burning hot.
He was very tired.
He closed his eyes.

While he was sleeping, Allah made
a big squash plant grow up very
quickly and lean over him to shade
him with its large, flat leaves.

When he woke up,
there were people
all around him.
They were talking in whispers.

"Where did he come from?"
"How did he get here?"

"There wasn't any squash plant on this beach before!"

"Who *is* he?"

"Look, he's moving!"

"Why, it's our old teacher Yunus ﷺ!"

"His god saved him! He must be right!"

"Let's carry him back to the city. We're going to listen to him carefully from now on!"

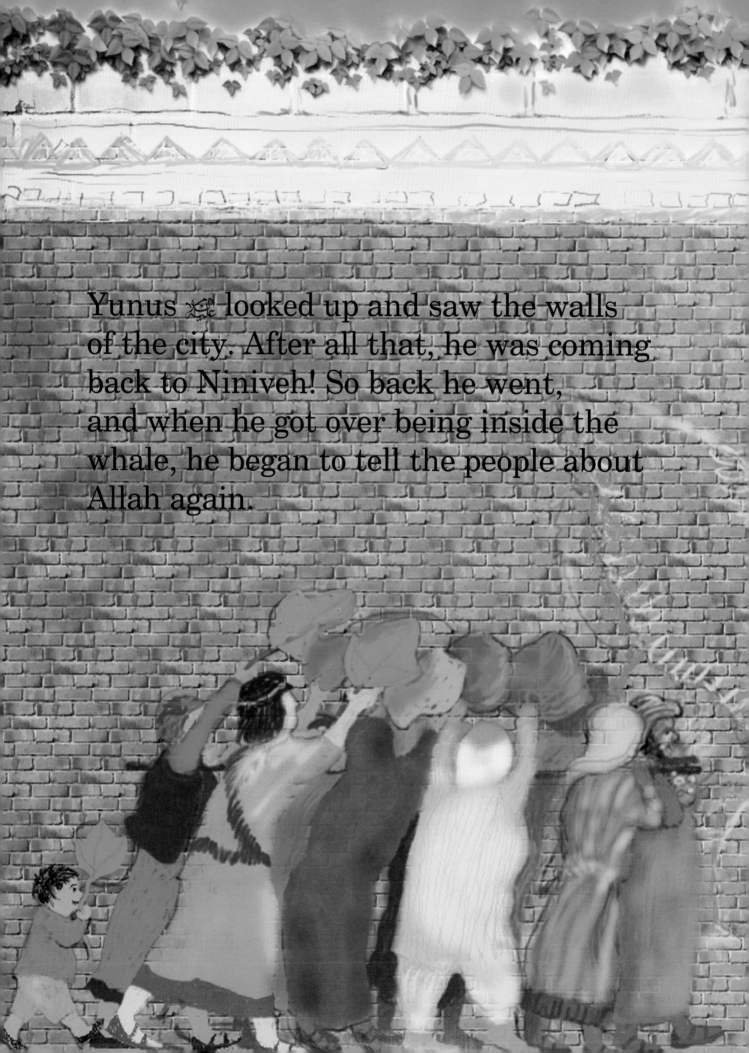

Yunus ﷺ looked up and saw the walls of the city. After all that, he was coming back to Niniveh! So back he went, and when he got over being inside the whale, he began to tell the people about Allah again.

They didn't argue any more. They listened carefully and they did what he said.

Allah forgave the people
for being so bad in the past.
For many years after that,
He blessed them
and their city
and
their prophet Yunus ﷺ
with good families,
good friends,
and a good life.

He blessed the whale, too.

The End